Black Bears

Written by
Michèle Dufresne

PIONEER VALLEY EDUCATIONAL PRESS, INC.

This is a black **bear**.
In a flash, the bear goes up the **tree**.

2

The black bear
is on a big rock.
He checks out the fish
that is swimming
in the **river**.

Can he get it? Yes!
Chomp! Chomp!
What a good snack
for the black bear.

Black bears eat berries,
roots, and fish. They also
prey on animals.

Oh no!

This black bear sees

a trash can.

The trash smells good
to the bear.
He is going to smash
the can.

Black bears can smell food from miles away.
Bears quickly learn that human trash makes an
easy meal. It is best to make trash inaccessible
to bears by bringing trash cans in at night.

Winter is coming.
The black bear is going
into her den.
She will spend all winter
in the den.

Black bears hibernate.
During this time, their body
temperature and heart rate
lower. They live off their
body fat all winter long.

Look at the small
black bear.

It is a cub.

The cub's mom
is going to get them
some fish for lunch.

A bear cub stays with its mother
for one and a half years while it
learns how to live on its own.

glossary

bear

tree

river

winter

12